15 Beads

JANE DUNNEWOLD

15 Beads

A Guide to Creating One-of-a-Kind Beads

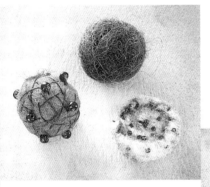

Martingale
& COMPANY

BOTHELL, WASHINGTON

ACKNOWLEDGMENTS

Thanks to all the students who have taken 15 Beads as a class or workshop. Without your generous sharing of information and discovery, this project could never happen. Thanks also to Melissa Lowe, my editor, and the staff of Martingale & Company, for encouragement, professional excellence, and a beautiful product. And thanks to John and Zenna, both of whom picked up the slack at home so I could get more done!

To the best girl in the world, Zenna James, and, of course, to John Carroll.

CREDITS

Technical Editor . . . . Melissa A. Lowe
Copy Editor . . . . Tina Cook
Design/Production Manager . . . . Cheryl Stevenson
Cover and Text Designer . . . . Trina Stahl
Illustrator . . . . Laurel Strand
Photographer . . . . Brent Kane

FIBER STUDIO PRESS

15 Beads: A Guide to Creating
One-of-a-Kind Beads
© 1998 by Jane Dunnewold
Martingale & Company
PO Box 118
Bothell, WA 98041-0118 USA

Printed in Hong Kong
03 02 01 00 99 98   6 5 4 3 2 1

Library of Congress Cataloging-in-Publication Data
Dunnewold, Jane
15 beads : a guide to creating one-of-a-kind
beads / Jane Dunnewold.
       p.   cm.
ISBN 1-56477-214-4
1. Beads.   2. Beadwork.   I. Title.
II. Title: Fifteen beads.
TT860.D86   1998
745.58'2—DC21   98-18137
                                                 CIP

The information in this book is presented in good faith, but no warranty is given nor results guaranteed. Since Martingale & Company has no control over choice of materials or procedures, the company assumes no responsibility for the use of this information.

MISSION STATEMENT
We are dedicated to providing quality products and service by working together to inspire creativity and to enrich the lives we touch.

Contents

Preface

ARTISTS AND QUILTMAKERS often discuss embellishing their work with beads. But the prices! My students and artist friends shared my dismay at the expense. These conversations planted the seed of an idea; I began to think about inexpensive ways to make my own beads.

Of course, the happiest consequence of a new idea is the time spent experimenting. I began to play with a vengeance! No material was left unconsidered. No craft-store aisle was ignored. When we discuss sources of inspiration, I always tell my students to "look up, look down, look all around." I took my own advice, and I did what any good teacher does when more information is required. I scheduled a class entitled "15 Beads" for the following semester.

The students didn't let me down. We played and played and played some more—for fifteen weeks. I learned as they learned, and was inspired as they shared their inspirations—15 Beads was official.

With more people using beads and embellishments to adorn their garments and quilts, making unique and highly personal beads seems to be an even more valid idea than it did when I first experimented. And so I offer it to you here. Play with a vengeance! Work with these beads until they become your own. Reflect, explore, and make some more.

Introduction

ORIGINALLY, *15 BEADS* meant learning how to make fifteen different types of beads during fifteen weeks of study. But the reference is a loose one. In reality, what you hold in your hands is a guide to many, many more than fifteen beads. This guide works best if you feel free to take the information and change it, stretch it, alter it, and add to it so that when you look at what you have made, you see your work—not mine!

After all, making beads one at a time, by hand, is labor intensive. If you just wanted beads for your current project, you could buy them. But buying something never gives us quite the satisfaction that making something does! With that in mind, consider this approach to get started: simply choose a bead or bead-making technique that appeals to you. Don't feel that you have to make something to coordinate with a current jewelry, garment, or quilt project. You can choose a bead just because you think the samples are pretty, or because the technique looks easy. Make a few beads, but don't hurry. Try to focus on the work at hand.

Artists often refer to staying focused as "centering." Centering is a freeing, anxiety-reducing way to work. If you focus on the bead under your fingers, without consciously thinking, "What should I do next?," your spirit will feel calm. And your busy unconscious will leap ahead for you—envisioning ideas and possibilities. Centering is one of the best things about making beads. When you are focused—fully engaged in the work before you—it's like meditating. Time will fly. Your mind will be refreshed, and you have the beads to thank.

That a process so simple can have so many rewards is a great gift. Make a bead, then make another bead. Each time, you have a start and a finish, a cycle completing itself. Feeling this rhythm and going with it frees you to contemplate the creative act, so consider this: each bead is a separate work of art. Center and begin and endeavor to make each bead as wonderful as possible. There is no failure! There is only the magic of the process.

Stay open and keep working. Before you know it, your pile of small delights will grow. Maybe they will never make it onto that quilt or jacket you intended to embellish. Maybe they will stay in a box, admired and cherished. The important thing will have been the thought time—the meditation each bead represents. You will succeed if some small portion of that thought time transcends the making of the bead and inserts itself into your daily life.

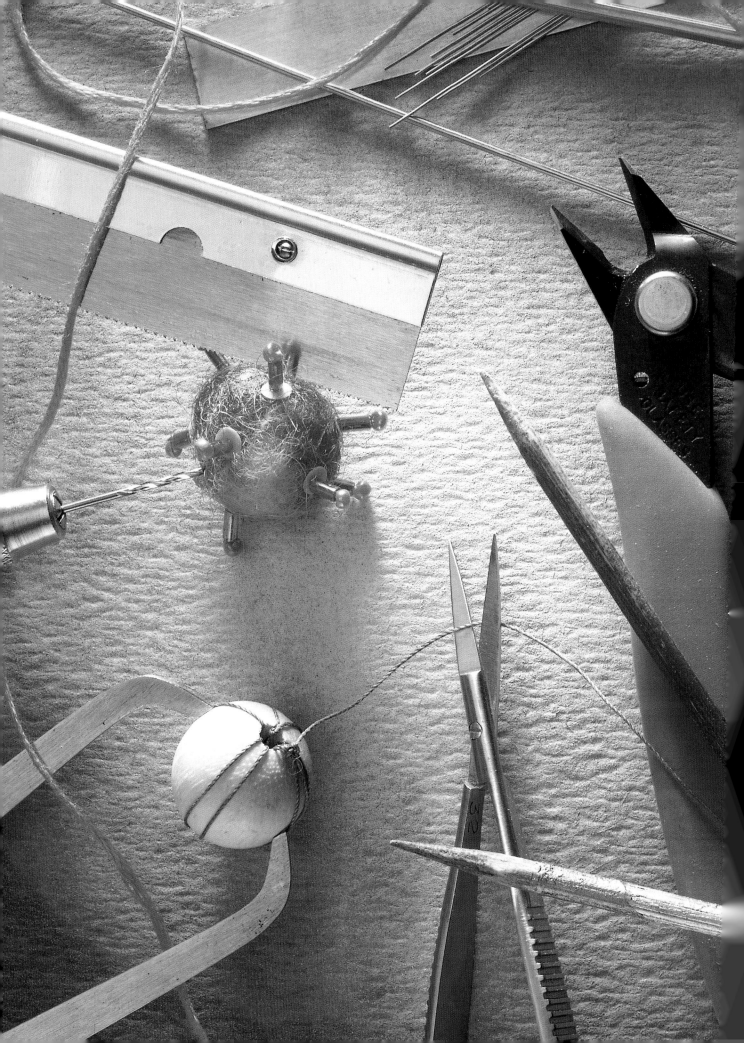

Materials and Tools

MOST OF THE beadmaking techniques and materials in this book are "innovative"—they include unexpected items that you may want to begin accumulating. (Most of us already have a head start on accumulating "stuff!") I list required materials and tools in the instructions for each technique, but you may want to begin gathering a variety of supplies for the techniques that most appeal to you. Look in art-supply, hardware, bead, fabric, and craft stores, as well as in mail-order catalogs. Don't rule anything out! A student in one of my workshops told me, with a certain amount of disdain, "Oh, but I never go into craft stores!" She considered herself an "Artist" and didn't recognize a craft store as the useful resource that it is. Keep your eyes open when you go shopping—no matter where you are. You'll be amazed at the products you'll discover and the ideas they'll generate.

Materials

THE FOLLOWING MATERIALS are useful for a variety of techniques. Specialized materials are listed with the appropriate beadmaking instructions.

Acrylic sealant: Spray cans of glossy and matte sealant are sold in art- and craft-supply stores.

Beads: Begin with painted and unpainted wooden beads in all sizes. You'll also want an assortment of inexpensive seed (round) and bugle (cylindrical) beads.

Craft paints: Try dimensional fabric paints and acrylic artists' paints in both tubes and bottles. Folkart, AppleBarrel, JonesTones, and Ceramcoat brands are versatile and long-lasting. Always look for paints that can be thinned with water—called water-based paints.

Gel medium: This is a thick, clear-drying product used to build up the surface of a painted canvas. It's sold in art-supply stores. Any brand will work. My favorite is Golden Self-Leveling Gel Medium. Choose shiny or matte finish based on your desired result.

Markers and pens: Collect different types and colors. Metallic markers look great. Be aware that many of these markers are not lightfast and will fade over time. If you can find permanent markers, buy them.

Metallic wax: Look for Rub and Buff, Treasure Gold, and Decorator's Gilt at craft-supply stores. You can rub these waxes, which are available in many colors, onto many different surfaces, and they are permanent when dry. Metallic waxes are a good way to finish paper edges and color wooden beads.

Papers: Collect any paper that attracts you—used gift wrap, origami, marbled, handmade, etc.

Polymer clay: Polymer clay comes in a wonderful array of colors and textures, all of which are intermixable. Brand names include Fimo (the most widely known), Super Sculpey, Sculpey III, Promat, Granitex, Super Elasticlay, Cernit, Modello, Formello, and Friendly Clay. The brands vary in how difficult each is to "condition," or soften, and in the strength of the finished material. I recommend starting with Sculpey III because it's easy to soften and readily available.

Threads: Look for sewing, beading, perle cotton, and fancy embroidery threads at fabric and craft stores.

Tools

THE FOLLOWING TOOLS are useful for a variety of beadmaking techniques. Specialized tools are listed with the appropriate beadmaking instructions.

Funnel: A small funnel makes putting beads back in small containers a snap!

Needles: Purchase beading, quilting (called "Betweens"), long Sharps, and Tapestry needles at fabric or craft stores.

Notebook: Keep a notebook for drawings and noting ideas and inspirations, and always travel with your notebook at hand. Don't let ideas get away!

Paintbrush: Match the scale of the brush to the scale of the project. Small brushes work best for small beads. I recommend high-quality brushes with natural bristles for detailed work.

Pliers: You will need small needle-nose and blunt-nose pliers for cutting wire and for folding wire and sheet metal.

Scissors: One pair of craft or paper scissors and one pair of good-quality fabric scissors.

Shoe boxes: Use shoe boxes to collect and hold materials and tools for a specific project.

Skewers: Purchase wooden skewers at the grocery store.

Small sauce dishes: These tiny bowls, available at Asian food markets, are a great way to contain beads as you work.

Storage containers: Recycle film canisters, baby-food bottles, and other containers to hold beads and other small stuff.

Swing-arm lamp: A swing-arm lamp or work light that you can position over your work surface is an important tool. It is much easier to do closeup work when you have the benefit of good lighting.

X-Acto knife and cutting surface: Use a thin, fine-tipped blade. The #11 blade is versatile; heavier blades can be cumbersome.

Homemade Tools

THERE ARE A variety of tools you can devise to help with beadmaking. For example, you need things to hold the beads as you paint or embellish them. With a little experimenting, you'll come up with all sorts of ways to hold the beads as you work. The following are my favorites:

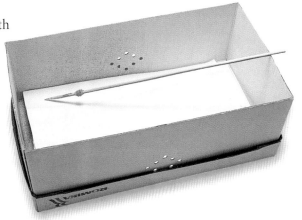

Long wooden skewers: Place tape or a rubber band about 1" from the tip of a wooden skewer. When you put a bead on the skewer, the tape or rubber band makes a "stop" that prevents the bead from sliding up and down the skewer as you paint. Place a bead on the skewer, then lay the skewer across an open shoe box or in a wide-mouth container.

Strawberry basket: Cut the rim off a strawberry basket (grocery stores package strawberries in these green plastic baskets). Place your beads on the spines to paint them or to let them dry.

Strawberry baskets are also ideal holders for groups of beads. You can see them through the openings in the basket and the plastic won't scratch the beads.

Egg carton: Push a 2" nail through the bottom of each cup in an egg carton, so the nails stick up when you turn the carton upside down. Place your beads on the nails to paint them or to let them dry.

Paper, Paint, and Wood

Rolled-Paper Beads

YOU CAN USE almost any light- to medium-weight paper to make rolled-paper beads. Origami paper, wrapping paper, handmade paper, and colorful magazine pages make lovely beads.

You Will Need

- Acrylic spray sealant
- Decorative papers
- Paintbrush
- Scissors or an X-Acto knife with a #11 blade (If you use an X-Acto knife, you'll also need a cutting surface.)
- Strawberry basket (see page 15)
- White glue or gel medium
- Wooden skewers

Making Beads

1. Try one of these shapes, or experiment with your own variations: From the paper, cut a long, skinny triangle, 1" wide or less at the base and at least 6" long, *or* cut a thin rectangle, 1" wide or less and about 6" long.

2. Using a paintbrush, spread a thin coating of white glue or gel medium on the wrong side of the paper. Leave about 1" at one end uncoated; this is the end you will use to begin rolling. If you are working with a triangle, make the dry area the base, not the point. If you forget to leave this dry area, the paper will stick to the skewer. Really stick! This is a mistake you make only once. *Wash your brush as soon as possible; if the glue dries, your brush will be ruined.*

3. Starting at the dry edge, roll the paper around the skewer, until you get to the area where the glue begins. Don't roll too tightly, or it will be hard to remove the completed bead from the skewer! As you roll, smooth out any excess glue with your fingers.

4. Slide the bead off the skewer, and place it on the spines of a strawberry basket to dry. When the glue is dry, lightly spray the bead with an acrylic sealant.

Hint

The thickness of the paper will affect the bead; heavy paper doesn't roll easily and makes a bulkier bead. Experiment to get a handle on the difference the paper weight can make.

Step 2

Step 3

EXPERIMENTING

♦ Make beads from plain white paper, then spray-paint them. Use spray paint and small stencils to create lovely patterns on the beads. Experiment with commercial stencils, paper doilies, and homemade stencils.

♦ Roll dry beads in white glue, then in fine glitter or seed beads.

♦ Wrap decorative thread around the middle of the bead several times, then tie it off. Experiment with different bead shapes and with stringing beads on the thread before wrapping the bead.

♦ Cut several different papers in diminishing sizes so that each paper shows over the last. Roll, then tie with decorative thread.

Paper-Covered Wooden Beads

LIGHTWEIGHT PAPERS ARE easiest to use for this bead style.

You Will Need

- ♦ Acrylic spray sealant (optional)
- ♦ Decorative papers
- ♦ Metallic wax (see page 13)
- ♦ Paintbrush
- ♦ Rubber bands or tape
- ♦ Scissors or an X-Acto knife with a #11 blade (If you use an X-Acto knife, you'll also need a cutting surface.)
- ♦ Shoe box or wide-mouth container
- ♦ Unfinished wooden beads, 1" or larger (larger beads are easier to use at first)
- ♦ White glue or gel medium
- ♦ Wooden skewers

Making Beads

1. Cut paper into thin strips or tiny squares (you may need to experiment to find the size that looks right for your beads). For best results, cut your squares ¼" or smaller. Large pieces won't lie flat on round beads.

2. Prepare wooden skewers with rubber bands or tape as described on page 15.

3. Place a wooden bead on a skewer, then use a paintbrush to cover the bead with a thin layer of white glue or gel medium.

4. Apply the paper strips or squares to the bead, laying them carefully across the surface. You can lay pieces side by side or overlap them.

5. Cover the entire bead surface with paper. Lay the skewer across an open shoe box or stand upright in a wide-mouth container, and allow the bead to dry.

6. To finish, rub metallic wax on any uncovered part (usually the ends). Follow the manufacturer's instructions for using the wax.

7. Spray with acrylic sealant if desired.

Hint

Go easy on the glue. Use too much, and your fingers will be wearing paper squares. Try coating the bead in sections, then using tweezers to place the paper pieces in the glue.

Step 1

Step 4

Step 6

EXPERIMENTING

♦ Cut a postage stamp into thin strips, then arrange the strips side by side around the bead. This works nicely on a long, oval bead. Use two stamps—they could be identical—to cover a 1" bead.

♦ Dip thread or perle cotton in glue, then wrap the glue-covered thread around a wooden bead, creating a pattern or texture on the surface. To create texture, cover the wrapped bead with small pieces of tissue paper, gluing until the thread and bead surface are no longer visible. You can paint and seal these beads when the glue is dry.

Painted Wooden Beads

UNFINISHED WOODEN BEADS of all shapes and sizes can sometimes be found in large bags of more than a hundred beads. Buy them! If you can't find these large bags, smaller bags of various shapes and sizes are sold in craft stores. If you can find only painted or varnished beads, you can remove the finish by putting the beads in a jar of turpentine overnight. This may not remove all the color, but it will dull the surface enough that it can be reworked.

You Will Need

- Rubber bands or tape
- Shoe box or wide-mouth container
- Unfinished wooden beads
- Wooden skewers

Making Beads

1. Prepare wooden skewers with rubber bands or tape as described on page 15.

2. Place a wooden bead on a skewer, then choose one of the following painting methods. When you are finished painting, lay the skewer across an open shoe box or stand upright in a wide-mouth container, and allow the bead to dry.

Craft Paints

Using a small paintbrush and craft paints (see page 12), hand paint the bead. To prevent color mixing, allow each color to dry before adding the next. Keep the bead on the skewer while it dries. If desired, finish with an acrylic spray sealant.

Dimensional Paints

Use dimensional paints (see page 15) straight from the tube or bottle. These paints are very thick and won't drip. Squeeze the color on and allow it to dry before adding more. These paints have glitter and metallic components that look great. They're so thick they can change the contour of the bead completely.

Markers and Pens

You can use a fine-tip marker or pen (see page 13) to draw an intricate design on the bead, then color the pattern with other pens. In general, begin with the

Using a fine-tip marker to draw a design.

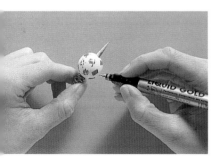

Using a metallic marker over a filled-in pattern.

OPPOSITE: *Hand-painted wooden beads by Julie Parker.*

lightest color, then apply darker colors, then metallics. Metallic markers are wonderful, but you must use these last; other pens won't cover metallic ink. To prevent bleeding, allow each color to dry before applying the next.

Stains and Dyes

Stains and dyes provide transparent color. Look for wood stains in hardware stores. Follow the manufacturer's instructions for using the stains on unfinished beads. Or use Rit fabric dye for similar effects. Make a concentrated batch of the dye, following the manufacturer's instructions. Place the beads and dye in a bottle for several hours, shaking the bottle often to dye the beads evenly (the beads will float). Apply sealant, if desired, especially if you want a high-gloss finish.

Spray Paints

Experiment with spray paints to make complex, colorful beads. You have to make some to appreciate how neat these look!

Work in a well-ventilated area, outside if possible. Use a dust mask to protect your lungs. Be sure to protect your work area with old newspapers.

1. String wooden beads onto a skewer (you don't need a stopper).

2. Hold the beads about a foot away from your body, at waist level. To get even color, lightly spray the paint at the skewer, turning it slowly as you spray to coat the beads evenly.

   If you spray heavily, the paint will begin to run. This is good! If you spray several colors consecutively, while all are wet, and you continue to turn the skewer, the paints will begin to bleed into one another. Metallics look fantastic when the colors mix this way.

   Stop spraying when the beads are well coated, but continue to turn the skewer until the paint sets, or there will be a noticeable drip on one side of the bead. After the paint sets, lay the skewer across an open box until the paint is completely dry.

Beads sprayed with one color of paint.

Beads sprayed with two colors of paint.

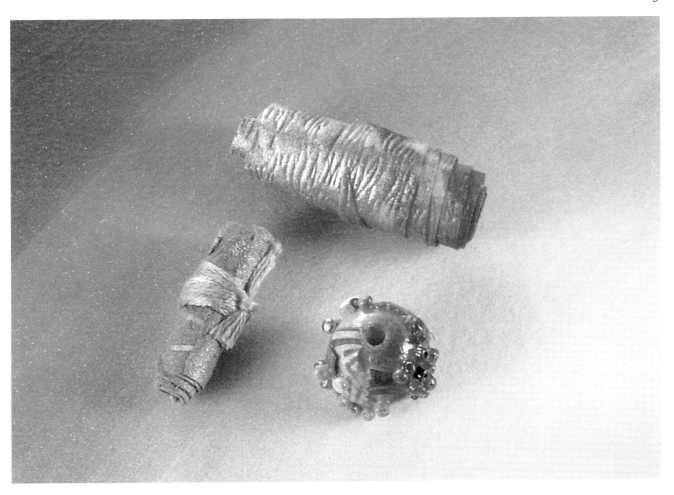

EXPERIMENTING

♦ Roll beads in glitter at the tacky stage of drying. For best results, spread the glitter in a shallow tray or pan. Place the bead or beads on a skewer, then roll them in the glitter tray.

♦ Sprinkle embossing powder (available at rubber-stamping and art- and craft-supply stores) onto the bead before the paint is completely dry. Use a heat gun (or a stove burner) to melt the embossing powder. The embossing powder swells to create a very hard, smooth surface. If you overheat or burn the embossing powder and paint, you create an organic look, similar to ceramic raku pottery.

Step 2

Marbling

You can marble wooden beads using Sumanigashi, a simple technique borrowed from Japanese papermakers.

1. Fill a large, shallow container with water so that you have a surface that is several inches across.

2. Using a toothpick, place drops of India ink or another permanent drawing ink on the surface of the water. (The drops should float *on top* of the water.) Swirl the surface slightly to pattern the ink.

3. Stick a wooden skewer or bobby pin into the end of a wooden bead, so you can hold the bead straight up and down.

4. Dip the bead into the surface of the ink and water, pushing it straight down until it is completely immersed, then pulling it up gently and evenly. The more ink you use, the heavier the pattern.

5. When the ink is dry, seal the bead with an acrylic spray.

Hint

Remember to sit up straight and use a good chair; bending or slumping over your work is hard on your body.

Paper-Maché Beads

PAPER-MACHÉ IS AN inexpensive, lightweight sculpting and modeling material made from paper pulp. You can make paper-maché from newspapers (see page 27), but buying shredded pulp speeds up the process and gives you a more uniform bead.

Beads created from paper-maché tend to look organic and natural, not as refined as beads made from wood or polymer clay.

You Will Need

- Celluclay or other packaged paper-maché material
- Craft or spray paints
- Dr. Scholl's foot smoother or fine sandpaper (The foot smoother is easy to hold and has both rough and fine surfaces.)
- Freezer bags (1-quart size)
- Gel medium
- Shoe box
- Small paintbrushes
- Vaseline
- Wooden skewers

Making Beads

1. Measure 2 cups of paper-maché material, ¼ cup gel medium, and ¾ cup warm water into a freezer bag. Seal the bag, then mix the ingredients by squeezing the bag. Squeeze until the material feels smooth and lump-free.

2. Make different bead shapes from the paper-maché, experimenting with balls, cylinders, and odd shapes. Use a wooden bead as a base if you want to ensure that your beads are a uniform size. Cover the bead with pulp, then roll it between the palms of your hands to smooth.

3. Grease several wooden skewers with Vaseline. To make holes, slowly *twist* a greased skewer through the center of each bead. Don't push the skewers through; this distorts the bead shape.

Step 1

Step 5

4. Lay the skewers across an open shoe box, and allow the beads to dry. It may take several days for the beads to dry completely. You can shorten the drying time by placing the beads in a 225°F oven for a few hours, but this may cause the beads to crack.

5. When the beads have dried, use Dr. Scholl's foot smoother or sandpaper to sand them smooth. Remember, paper-maché will always look organic compared to other types of beads.

6. Paint the beads with craft or spray paints as described on pages 20–23. You can make some terrific faux rocks to string and wear!

Homemade Paper Maché

You Will Need

- Blender
- 1 tablespoon linseed oil
- 2 tablespoons spackle
- 2 tablespoons white glue
- 16 sheets of newspaper
- 2-quart pot
- Sieve

Hint

*Don't shorten the
soaking or cooking
time; the pulp will
be harder to handle.*

Making Paper-Maché

1. Tear the newspaper into 1" squares. Place the squares in the pot, then cover with hot water. Soak overnight.

2. Place the pot on the stove and heat the paper-water mixture to a full boil. Boil for 1 hour. Add water as needed to keep the paper covered and at a rolling boil.

3. Strain the paper through a sieve.

4. Blend the paper in batches. Place about 1 cup in a blender. Add just enough water to cover the paper. Blend until the fibers are broken up. Pour the pulp into a sieve. Use your hand to squeeze out most of the water. The pulp works best if it is damp.

5. Mix 2 cups of pulp with the linseed oil, spackle, and white glue. When the mixture is smooth and lump-free, you can use it to make beads as described on pages 25–26.

EXPERIMENTING

- Use premixed wall grout to smooth out the surface of your beads after they've dried. Fill in any irregularities by spreading the grout with a toothpick or plastic knife, then rolling the bead in your hand. Dry on a skewer.

- Several companies offer acrylic paints for decorating glass and ceramics. Consider using these to make your beads stronger and longer lasting. Paint the beads, then "fire" them in your oven following the manufacturer's instructions. Look for glass and ceramic paints in craft stores.

Cloth

Felt Beads

FELTING IS THE PROCESS of working wool in hot and cold water, with soap and a great deal of agitation. In response, the wool fibers compress to create a compact, nonraveling fabric. I've included two techniques for making felt beads: from unspun wool by hand and from recycled wool clothing with a washing machine.

FELTING BY HAND

FOR THIS TECHNIQUE, you use wool roving—loose, unspun wool—to make a bead. Wool roving feels much like synthetic pillow stuffing. You can find wool roving in shops that carry weaving supplies, or you can order it from one of the resources on page 76. Experiment with the natural colors—cream, white, brown, and black—as well as with dyed colors. Brightly dyed wool makes great beads!

You Will Need

- 1 tray of ice cubes
- 2 basins or plastic dishpans
- Dishwashing liquid
- Dollmaker's needle
- Old nylon stocking (optional)
- Wool roving

Making Beads

1. Pour 1 capful of dishwashing liquid into a basin. Add boiling water until the basin is half full.

2. Empty 1 tray of ice cubes into the second basin. Add cold water until the basin is half full.

3. From the wool roving, pull off a hank about 3 times larger than the desired size of your finished bead. Shred the wool by pulling it apart loosely several times.

   The bead may develop cracks if the wool is not adequately shredded before you begin immersing it. If your bead cracks when dry, embellish it to hide the crack, and pull the wool more for your next beads.

4. Immerse the wool in the basin of hot water, removing it as soon as it is wet. It will be hot! Roll the wet wool between the palms of your hands several times—as though you were rolling a ball of clay—to form a bead.

5. Immerse the bead in the ice water long enough to saturate it. A quick dunking should be adequate. Continue rolling it between your palms. It may help to count slowly to 30 each time you switch from cold to hot water, rolling, counting, dunking again, and so on.

Steps 1 and 2

Step 3

Step 4

Step 6

Hint

Mix colors by pulling out more than one color when you choose your hank. Pull the wool apart in a shredding motion to mix the colors prior to immersing the wool the first time.

Some wools reduce more quickly than others, so you may find that your wools felt at different rates. You may like the irregular look this produces, or you may prefer to use wools that felt at about the same rate.

6. Alternate rolling the bead in the basins of hot and cold water, until the wool feels very dense. You can expect to work on each bead for several minutes.

7. Squeeze the bead to remove any remaining water. Allow the bead to air dry, or place several beads in an old nylon stocking. Loosely tie the end, then dry in a clothes dryer on a high heat setting. The heat will compact the wool further.

8. Use the dollmaker's needle to pierce and string your felt beads. It is long enough to pierce several beads at once.

FELTING BY MACHINE

YOU CAN MAKE felt beads by recycling wool fabrics, such as old sweaters and skirts. The process is much like that described for felting by hand, but you use a washing machine and a clothes dryer.

You Will Need

- 100% wool fabric (Be sure to check the fabric content on the label.)
- Dishwashing liquid
- Masking tape
- Permanent fabric glue
- Scissors
- Steam iron

EXPERIMENTING

- Embroider your beads. French knots, bullion knots, and the buttonhole stitch look great worked in bright colors on deeply colored wool. For more information, see pages 43–51.

- Embellish your beads. The beauty of stitching on wool beads is that you can sew right through the middle of the bead to move from spot to spot. You may want to make a "treasure" bead to be used as a focal point on a necklace or a garment. Embellish a bead with smaller beads, charms, or other materials.

- Use round felted beads as buttons. Sew right through the back to create a shank.

- Combine a felted bead with a tassel, either commercial or handmade. To attach a bead to a tassel, pull the top thread or loop of the tassel through the middle of the bead. To attach a bead to a commercial tassel, pull the cord through the bead center.

Step 4

Making Beads

1. Place the wool fabric in a washing machine with ¼ cup dishwashing liquid. Set the machine for hot wash, cold rinse.

2. Repeat the wash and rinse cycle at least 4 times, or until the wool has reduced and will no longer ravel or fray. When the wool has been properly reduced, you won't be able to see the original weave. Dry the fabric in the dryer on high heat.

3. Iron the wool, using steam to help smooth it flat.

4. Cut 1" x 3" rectangles or triangles with 1" sides from the wool. (You can also cut these into rounds and skip the next step.)

5. Spread permanent fabric glue on one side of a wool shape, then roll it up. Use masking tape to hold the roll closed until the glue dries. You can embellish these rolled beads, use them as buttons, or string them for jewelry.

Pillow Beads

PILLOW BEADS ARE aptly named—they look like little pillows! These beautiful, versatile beads are a great way to use fabric scraps. Use interesting fabrics if you want interesting beads.

You Will Need

- Assorted fabric scraps, each at least 8" x 10"
- Embroidery hoop (optional)
- Embroidery threads
- Scissors
- Sewing machine (optional)
- Sewing thread and needle
- Small beads and charms (optional)
- Small package Polyfiberfill stuffing

Making Beads

1. From a fabric scrap, cut strips *at least* 2" x 4". This technique goes faster if you cut long rectangles of fabric, rather than cutting a bead length at a time. Once you make a bead, you will know how wide you want your beads, and hence, your fabric, to be.

2. If desired, embroider your fabric—by hand or by machine—*before* sewing the rectangles into tubes. Use an embroidery hoop to stabilize the fabric.

   If you want to add small beads and heavy embroidery threads, complete the remaining steps before embellishing. It is easier to sew the rectangles into tubes if you aren't running into beads in the seam allowance!

3. Fold the strip in half lengthwise, wrong sides together. Align the long edges, and finger-press the fold to form a crease.

Hint

If you hand stitch beads and charms onto fabric beads, you may want to hide the thread ends. Knot the thread, make a stitch through the Polyfiberfill, then tug on the thread to pop the knot through the fabric. Trim the thread end.

OPPOSITE: *Pillow bead necklace by Cheryl Kalter. Embroidered and beaded by hand.*

Step 4

Step 5

4. Cut a piece of embroidery thread at least 2" longer than the fabric rectangle. Lay the thread inside the strip so that it lies in the fold, with the ends extending beyond the short raw edges.

5. Beginning on the folded side, as shown, sew a short raw edge of the folded rectangle, catching the embroidery thread and using a ¼"-wide seam allowance. At the corner, turn and continue stitching down the long side. Stop stitching at the edge of the long side.

6. Gently pull the embroidery thread, easing the sewn end into the tube. Pull until the tube turns right side out.

7. Trim the seam allowance close to the stitching, then remove the embroidery thread. Lay the thread aside to use on the next tube.

8. Cut the tube into bead lengths, adding 1" to the desired finished length so you can turn under the ends.

9. On one of the lengths cut in step 8, turn under the raw edge ½". Using a needle and thread, baste the fold as shown. (Sewing along the fold gives the bead ends the cleanest finish.) When you have basted around the tube, tightly gather the thread to close the tube end. Knot the thread ends and trim.

10. Push the Polyfiberfill into the open end of the tube to fill it. Turn under the raw edge, then stitch and gather as described in step 9. Embellish with beads and charms, if desired. Voilà!

Step 8

Step 9

EXPERIMENTING

♦ **Make beads from ribbon instead of fabric, then embellish with seed beads.**

♦ **Use pre-embellished fabrics, such as embroidered linens.**

♦ **Make beads from patterned fabric, then embroider over the pattern.**

♦ **Make an elaborate pillow bead, then make a coordinating tassel. This could be the focal point of a necklace, the closure on a garment, or a lovely object in its own right!**

Gallery Show

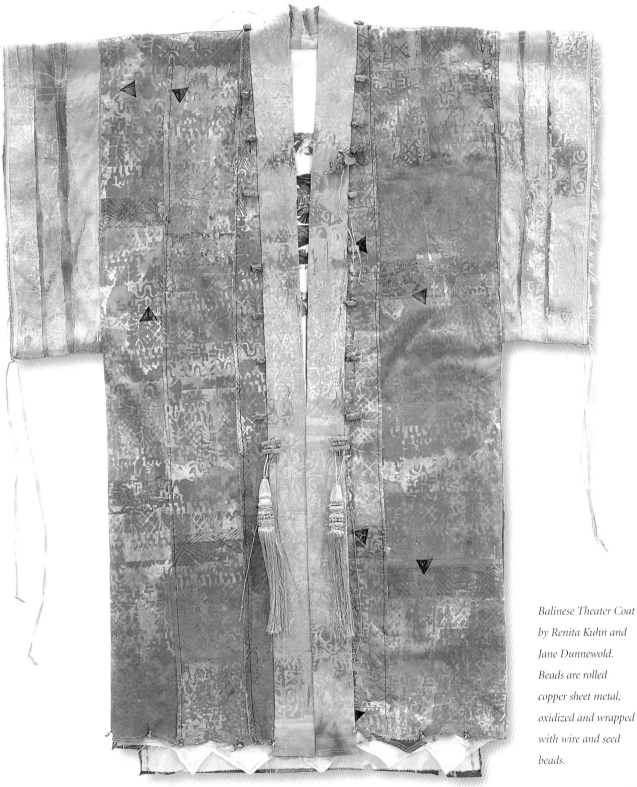

Balinese Theater Coat
by Renita Kuhn and
Jane Dunnewold.
Beads are rolled
copper sheet metal,
oxidized and wrapped
with wire and seed
beads.

37

Beaded bracelet by Jane Dunnewold.
Wrapped and peyote-stitched base
with commercial beads, wrapped
beads over a wooden bead base, and
buttonhole-stitched beads.

Bracelet by Jane Dunnewold. Friendly
Plastic and commercial beads.

*Bracelet by Elinor Dunnewold. Polymer
clay beads with inlaid clay circles.*

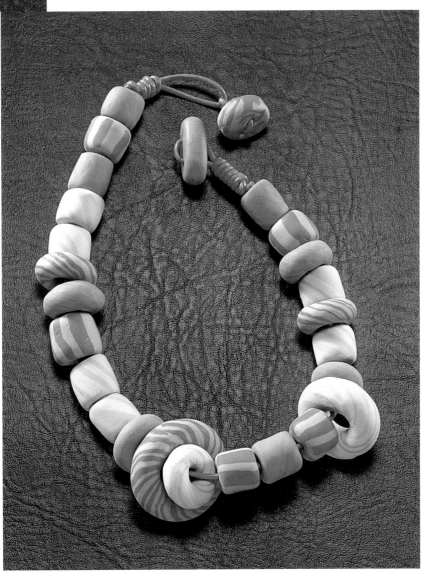

*Necklace by Alison Whittemore.
Polymer clay beads.*

Beads by Joanne Laessig. Wrapped beads over a bead core.

Necklace by Jane Dunnewold. Wrapped beads over a cotton core, with commercial beads and wrapped and embroidered beads.

Thread

THE FOLLOWING TECHNIQUES embellish wooden beads in several ways. You may want to bone up on your embroidery skills!

Wrapped Beads

YOU MAY WANT to use a painted bead for this technique, because the wooden base will show. The thread you use will also show, so choose an attractive, strong thread that you really like. Be sure your thread won't break easily—metallic thread and lightweight sewing thread are not good choices. Rub beeswax on thin threads to strengthen them.

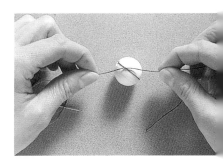

Base thread

You Will Need

+ Beading needles, or needles small enough for seed beads
+ Beading thread, heavy sewing thread, or #8 perle cotton
+ Colored wooden beads in assorted sizes
+ Seed beads
+ Small dishes to hold beads
+ White glue or clear nail polish

Making Beads

1. Thread a needle with approximately 15" of thread (longer threads may tangle and knot). Draw the needle and thread through the hole in a wooden bead. Tie the thread around the bead, pulling it tight and knotting it securely. Put a drop of glue or nail polish on the knot to secure it. Trim the thread.

2. Pull the knot into the bead hole so it doesn't show. This is the *base thread.*

3. Using the needle and thread, make a buttonhole stitch around the base thread near one end, as shown. Think of this as the top of the bead. Your stitching secures the thread so that beads won't slide into the hole. *Begin every row with a buttonhole stitch over the base thread.*

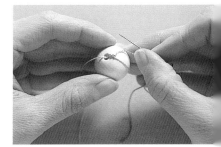

Step 1

Step 3

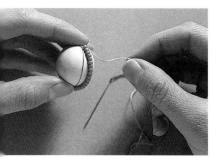

Step 4

Step 6

4. Working from the top of the bead, string seed beads on the thread until you can wrap the wooden bead from one hole to the other. Count the seed beads. (If you use beads of different sizes for each wrap, you'll have to experiment each time.)

5. When you have determined how many beads it will take to make 1 wrap, lay the beads against the base thread and buttonhole-stitch around the base thread at the bottom of the bead.

6. Run the needle up through the center of the wooden bead, and buttonhole-stitch around the base thread as described in step 2. Always buttonhole-stitch before stringing beads on the thread. String seed beads on the thread, then wrap the wooden bead, laying the thread next to the previous wrap.

7. Repeat steps 3–6, making as many or as few wraps as you like. To completely cover the wooden bead, wrap strands until the surface no longer shows.

8. If the thread at the bead ends is more obvious than you would like, stitch beads around the openings to cover the thread.

Hint

To add thread:

1. Trim the original thread, leaving a tail at least 2" long. (Shorter lengths will drive you crazy.)

2. Cut a length of thread 18" longer than you need.

3. Tie the threads together, sliding the knot as far onto the original thread as possible.

4. Tug on the new thread while simultaneously tugging the original thread until you hear a little pop. The threads will now be knotted so tightly they won't come undone. Test by tugging gently on the new thread to make sure it won't pull off.

This knotting technique usually makes a knot that is small enough to pull inside a seed bead. If the knot won't fit inside a seed bead, hide it by covering it with the next wrap.

EXPERIMENTING

♦ Use bugle beads on a cylindrical or oblong bead. Combine bugle beads with seed beads for a regal look.

♦ Cover the wooden bead with tiny red, purple, or black beads. The finished bead will look like a berry!

LEFT: *Necklace by Jane Dunnewold. Wrapped beads over a cotton core, with commercial beads and wrapped and embroidered bead embellishments.*

Buttonhole-Stitched Beads

THESE BEADS CAN look regular or irregular—they're charming either way. Work loosely to start; it's easier to see what you're doing if you don't pack in too many beads. Your base bead may show, so choose a bead and thread you want to see.

You Will Need

- Beading needles, or needles small enough for seed beads
- Funnel for returning beads to their containers when you're finished
- #8 perle cotton, beading thread, or heavy sewing thread (Perle cotton works particularly well for this technique.)
- Seed beads
- Scissors
- Small dishes to hold beads
- White glue or clear nail polish
- Wooden beads (1" diameter and larger are easiest to use)

Making Beads

1. Thread a needle with approximately 15" of thread (a longer thread may tangle and knot), then draw the needle and thread through the hole in the wooden bead. Tie the thread around the bead, pulling it tight and knotting it securely. Put a drop of glue or nail polish on the knot to secure it. Trim thread.

2. Pull the knot into the bead so it doesn't show. This is the *base thread*.

3. Using the needle and thread, make a buttonhole stitch around the base thread near one hole, as shown on page 43. Think of this as the top of the bead. Your stitching secures the thread so that beads won't slide into the hole. Do not trim the thread.

4. Hold the bead so that your sewing thread is on your left. The base thread should be horizontal across the bead as you hold it.

5. Pick up a seed bead with the needle, then slide it down the thread so that it's next to the wooden bead.

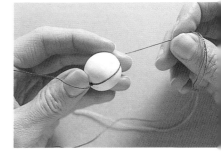

Step 4

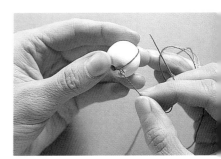

Step 5

Step 6

Step 7

Step 9

Step 10

6. Buttonhole-stitch around the base thread, then pull the thread tight. The seed bead will lie against the base thread, held in place by the buttonhole loop.

7. Repeat steps 4–6 until you have a line of combined stitches and seed beads running the length of the wooden bead.

8. Run the needle up the center of the wooden bead, to the left of the base thread, then buttonhole-stitch around the base thread.

9. Begin the second row of beading. This time, do not stitch around the original base thread. Instead, stitch into the loops you made when you attached each bead on the first wrap. After you put the seed bead on your thread, slide it down so that it lies flat against the wooden bead and next to the first row of seed beads as shown.

10. Make a buttonhole stitch through the loop directly above the bead. Pull it snug, add another bead, and continue working, always adding a bead and then making a buttonhole stitch through the loop just above the bead you added.

    The beads will not lie in a straight line against the base bead unless you tug slightly on the sewing thread every time you make a stitch. As you stitch, check to be sure the thread isn't caught on any of the seed beads.

11. Continue stitching rows of beads as described in steps 9–10, stitching every row into the loops of the row before it. When you have worked enough rows to cover half of the wooden bead, pull on the stitching. You should be able to stretch it out slightly so you can see the net of beads you're creating. Continue stitching rows of beads until you can stretch the net all the way around the bead.

12. To finish, stitch through the original base thread. This will keep the beads in place so that they cover the entire base.

Hint

The sewing thread should always be to the right of the bead you added last. If you look carefully, you may see that the thread is getting caught around a bead or two in a row you have completed. This keeps it from holding the bead you just added firmly in place. If you are seeking uniformity, watch your thread and work slowly until you get the technique figured out.

It also helps to be consistent when you hold the base bead. Kept the left the left and the right the right. It's easy to become confused if you change back and forth or switch the bead up and down while you work.

EXPERIMENTING

- Use beads of different sizes for an organic look.

- Alternate your stitches, adding beads to some but not to others.

- Use a felted wool bead (see page 29) instead of a wooden bead.

- Add dimension with bugle beads, stitched so that they stand out from the bead:

1. As you begin a buttonhole stitch, slide a bugle bead down to the wooden base bead.

2. Add a seed bead, sliding it down the thread so it rests against the top of the bugle bead.

3. Run your needle back through the bugle bead, and pull the thread tight. The seed bead will sit on top of the bugle bead. Don't sew through the seed bead by mistake—it will come off!

4. Buttonhole-stitch as described on page 43, gently sliding the thread so that the bugle stays upright against the wooden bead base. The bugle will stand out from the bead's surface, topped with the seed-bead anchor.

Spider-Web Beads

THIS IS VARIATION on a classic embroidery stitch. Easy enough for children!

You Will Need

- ♦ #8 perle cotton, beading thread, or heavy sewing thread (perle cotton works particularly well for this technique)
- ♦ Needle
- ♦ Scissors
- ♦ Seed beads
- ♦ Small dishes to hold beads
- ♦ White glue or clear nail polish
- ♦ Wooden beads, 1" diameter or larger

Making Beads

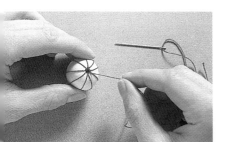

Step 4

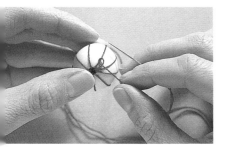

Step 5

Step 6

1. Thread a needle with approximately 15" of thread (a longer thread may tangle and knot).

2. Draw the needle and thread through the hole in the wooden bead. Tie the thread around the bead, pulling it tight and knotting it securely. Do not trim the thread. Put a drop of white glue or clear nail polish on the knot to secure it.

3. Pull the knot into the bead so it doesn't show. This is a *base thread*.

4. Repeat steps 2–3 until you have 6 or 8 evenly spaced base threads. You may need more base threads for bigger beads. A 1"-diameter bead will be fine with 6.

5. Hold the wooden bead so the openings are at the top and bottom. Buttonhole stitch (see page 43) around a base thread at the top. This keeps the seed beads from sliding into the middle of the bead.

6. To create the spider web, you stitch around the base threads one at a time. Pick up a seed bead with your needle. Slide it down against the wooden bead, then slide the needle under the first base thread to the left. Do not sew through the base thread, just slide under it. Bring the needle around and slide it under the base thread again, so the base thread is wrapped once in the sewing thread.

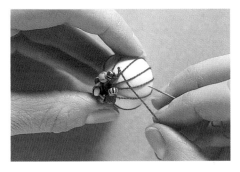 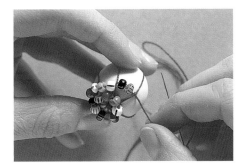

Step 7   *Step 8*

7. Keep moving to the left, adding beads as described in step 6. Always move in the same direction.

8. When you have stitched back to the first base thread, simply drop down slightly and continue, gradually spiraling around the bead. Because the distance between the base threads increases as you work toward the middle of the bead, you need to add 1 or more beads to each row. For example, use 1 bead per wrap for the top row, 2 beads for the second row, 3 beads for the third row, and so on. Work in reverse from the middle of the bead to the bottom.

Hint

Take time to look at how the stitches are made. When you see that the thread always wraps in the same direction and "points" where to go next, the stitch becomes simple.

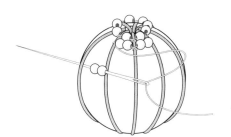

EXPERIMENTING

♦ **Vary your bead sizes for a wonderfully irregular treasure bead.**

♦ **Work a bead entirely in threaded spider web, minus the beads. This is an interesting variation and makes great buttons.**

Polymer Clay

POLYMER CLAY IS actually synthetic clay made from polyvinyl chloride (PVC). It is readily available, easy to work, easy to "cure," or harden, and the finished beads are very durable. If you have never worked with polymer clay, start with Sculpey III. And if you like this medium, look for one or more of the books devoted entirely to polymer clay. (See "Recommended Reading" on page 78.) The beads you see here are only an introduction to an exciting, multifaceted material.

You Will Need

- Aluminum pie plate
- Clear acrylic sheet, at least 10" x 14", to use as a work surface
- Oven thermometer
- Polymer clay (3 or 4 colors)
- Razor blade, scalpel, or tissue-slicing blade
- Wooden skewers

Making Beads

1. Break off a chunk of clay. The size you take will be about the same size as the bead you make; the clay will not compress or change in volume.

    If you want a particular color not found premixed, try mixing two or more colors to get the color you have in mind.

2. The clay may be too stiff to work at first. To condition the clay, warm it by holding it in your hands, or knead it. *Do not* try to soften clay in a conventional or microwave oven—it will harden it instead!

3. Form the chunk of clay into a ball by rolling it gently and evenly between your palms. This is the best way to get a nice, round bead.

Step 3

OPPOSITE: *Polymer clay beads by Elinor Dunnewold.*

Hint

Most of the polymer-clay colors you can buy are "pure hues," or bright, true colors. If you want a pastel or a tint, add white. If you want a shade or a tone of a color, add a bit of black. Store unused clay in a box or boxes, sorted by color. The clay will not harden over time, and the box will keep dust out. To roll out softened clay, use a dowel or an acrylic rod.

4. There are many ways to embellish or pattern polymer clay beads. Try the following, or see "Experimenting" for more ideas.

    a. Roll out a "snake" (see page 55) of a different-colored clay.

    b. Use a razor blade, scalpel, or tissue-slicing blade to slice uniform rounds from one end of the snake. To avoid distortion, don't press the blade down; gently rock it back and forth.

    c. Press the rounds of clay onto the beads, then roll the bead so that the rounds flatten into the surface.

    Always pattern your beads before making the holes; otherwise the beads may become distorted.

5. Use the wooden skewer to make a hole in your bead. Twist, rather than push, the skewer through the bead. The twisting motion makes a uniform hole and keeps the bead from becoming distorted.

6. Place several beads of the same size on a skewer, then lay the skewer across the pie plate. If you bake beads on the pie plate, they will have flat spots. Cure your beads in a conventional home oven, and use an oven thermometer to check for an accurate temperature. *Do not* try using a microwave oven to cure polymer clay.

    Refer to the manufacturer's instructions for the curing temperature. As a general rule:

    ♦ Bake small beads, about 1" in diameter, for 10 minutes at 275°F.

    ♦ Bake medium beads, about 2" in diameter, for 12 minutes at 275°F.

    ♦ Bake beads larger than 2" in diameter for 15 minutes at 275°F.

    If the bead turns brown as it bakes, the oven is too hot. Do not heat beads to more than 300°F. Cut down the time the beads spend in the oven. The clay should not lose its original color.

7. These beads do not need to be sealed, but if you would like a shiny finish, check the spray acrylic you intend to use. It should say whether it is compatible with polymer clay. Those not compatible with polymer clay will ruin the bead. Several polymer clay manufacturers also make glazes and varnishes.

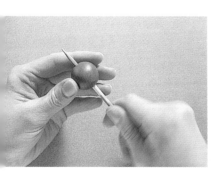

Step 5

EXPERIMENTING

♦   Roll tiny balls of clay and stick them to a larger, different-colored bead. These are referred to as "eye beads."

♦   Roll tiny balls of clay, stick them to a larger, different-colored bead, then roll the bead between your palms. The balls will turn into wonderful spots! Try adding spots of more than one color.

♦   Make beads in shapes other than balls. Try cylinders, squares, and odd shapes.

♦   Apply composition metal leaf. Lay a small piece of the leaf against the bead and roll it into the surface. This looks great with translucent clay.

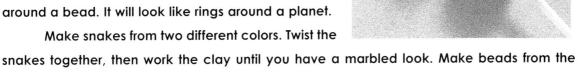

♦   Wrap a small tile in newspaper. Using a hammer, break the tile into small pieces. Stick the pieces into a clay bead before baking. Instant mosaic!

♦   Roll a ball into a snake, working up and down the shape evenly until it is long and thin. Use the part of your hands next to your fingers to do the rolling.

Trim a small section of the snake and wrap it around a bead. It will look like rings around a planet.

Make snakes from two different colors. Twist the snakes together, then work the clay until you have a marbled look. Make beads from the marbled clay.

Wrap a snake around a bead, then roll it between your palms. The snake turns into stripes.

♦   Try photo transfers.
   1. Photocopy small images (or reduce large images).
   2. Before baking your bead, smooth a photocopy against it until the paper lies flat against the surface. Wait for 45 minutes, then carefully peel away the copy paper. The image should transfer to the clay and will be permanent once baked.

Friendly Plastic

FRIENDLY PLASTIC IS a heat-sensitive plastic available in bright colors, jewel tones, metallics, and prints. Because it melts at a low temperature, you can shape it by hand. The plastic hardens as it cools, and the finished beads look like glass. It is tough, but never, never leave these beads in a hot car, or subject them to heat once they're completed. They will melt!

You Will Need

- 2-quart saucepan
- Cooking spray
- Friendly Plastic, in all kinds of colors
- Metal spatula or large spoon (This must be metal.)
- Scissors
- Wide-mouth container
- Wooden beads, 1" diameter or larger (Unfinished beads work best, but you can use sandpaper to roughen painted beads.)
- Wooden skewers

Making Beads

1. If you are using a 1"-diameter bead, cut a 1" square of Friendly Plastic. As a rule, you need a piece of plastic big enough to melt and stretch up and around the bead. To figure out whether I'm cutting a big enough square, I think of wrapping the bead by pulling up the four corners of the square as if it were cloth. Don't worry, you can always add more Friendly Plastic. This is a very forgiving process.

Step 1

2. Fill the saucepan three-quarters full with water. Heat the water to a simmer, then lower the temperature to medium heat. The water will slowly evaporate. Add more water as needed—you should be able to immerse the spoon without the plastic falling off. If the temperature is too high, the plastic will get too soft and become hard to control.

Hint

You can reheat the plastic-wrapped bead as often as you like, but metallics may become dull.

If your bead is not completely covered with plastic, cut small pieces of plastic in either the same color you were using or in different colors. Heat the pieces on the spatula, then stick them on the plastic-wrapped bead. Reheat the bead as described below, then roll the bead between your palms to smooth it.

If your piece of Friendly Plastic was too big, the excess may fill the bead holes. Cut a smaller piece next time. If you can't find the holes to clear them, prick the bead all over with a wooden skewer until you locate them. Reheat the bead and smooth out the marks. If you can't easily clear the holes with the skewer, you may need to discard the bead and start again.

You may get air bubbles between the plastic and the wooden bead. If you have trouble smoothing them out, use a needle to poke a hole in the plastic, then smooth it flat.

3. Lightly mist the metal spatula or spoon with cooking spray. The cooking spray keeps the plastic from sticking to the utensil.

4. Place the plastic square on the spatula and lower it just below the surface of the water. (Be sure to hold the spatula so the square doesn't slide off.) Slowly count to 20.

5. Remove the plastic square from the water, then use your fingers to pull and stretch it around a wooden bead, leaving the holes open. Work quickly so the plastic doesn't cool. The plastic should pull smoothly and wrap evenly. If you are having trouble stretching the plastic, it isn't hot enough. If necessary, put the bead on a wooden skewer and dip it into the hot water to reheat.

6. Roll the plastic-covered bead between your palms to smooth it. Try not to fill in the bead holes. If necessary, use a wooden skewer to clear the holes.

7. Once the bead feels smooth, place it on a wooden skewer and stand the skewer in a wide-mouth container until the bead cools.

Step 6

EXPERIMENTING

♦ Stick small pieces of Friendly Plastic to a warm bead. Save excess bits and pieces for embellishing other beads.

♦ Cut a skinny piece of Friendly Plastic, and heat it on a spatula. Stick one end to a plastic-wrapped bead, then pull and stretch the heated strip, wrapping it loosely around the bead so it looks like the rings of Saturn.

♦ Make a mosaic bead. Collage tiny pieces of Friendly Plastic onto a warm plastic-wrapped bead. Try jewel-tone bits on a black background; the contrast makes the jewel colors gleam.

♦ Wrap a postage stamp around a warm plastic-wrapped bead. Roll the bead between your palms, smoothing the stamp onto the Friendly Plastic. To work the stamp into the plastic, apply pressure as you roll. Use an acrylic spray sealant to permanently seal the stamp to the bead.

♦ Collage small paper scraps to a warm, plastic-wrapped bead. Roll the bead between your palms and seal as described above.

♦ Make a tube or cylindrical bead by using a short length of plastic drinking straw as a base. Cut a strip of Friendly Plastic, then heat as described above. Wrap the strip around the drinking straw and embellish. Roll the plastic so that it extends just beyond the edges of the straw.

♦ Use Friendly Plastic to dress up old buttons. Cut tiny snippets of plastic and lay them on the button. (Don't cover the holes.) Place the button on an aluminum pie plate, then heat for 5 minutes in a 250°F oven. The plastic will melt onto the button, changing it completely!

♦ For beads that look like glass, finish with a high-gloss acrylic sealant.

Found Objects

TUNE IN TO discover bead and embellishment possibilities in the world around you. Look for "found objects"—bottle caps, seeds, watch parts, stones, small mirrors—you can incorporate into beaded works. These objects add unusual and personal elements to your work and should be highly prized.

Making Beads

Use these ideas to turn your found objects into beads.

♦ Use a thin nail, needle, or drill to make holes in found objects. Use the smallest drill bit available. To keep shells from cracking, put a few drops of water on the surface while drilling.

♦ If you can't pierce an object, use E6000 adhesive (available at craft and art-supply stores) to glue button shanks or wire loops to it.

♦ For best results, spray seed pods and other fragile objects with acrylic sealant before using. Store them with a mothball to keep away unwanted creatures. You may also want to seal rusty metal.

♦ Dampen paper and press it onto the button form of a button-covering set. Fold the edges to the back, then pop the metal shank onto the back. Allow the paper to dry. To finish, spray the dry paper button with an acrylic sealant.

♦ Oxidize metal buttons and other objects, following the directions on pages 68–69.

♦ Coat the top of a large button with E6000 adhesive or premixed grout. Make a mosaic by pressing bits of found materials into the adhesive or grout for terrific one-of-a-kind buttons!

Metal

IN MOST CASES, these beads will stand up to hand washing, but dry cleaning may strip the metallic finish. If in doubt, ask a dry cleaner to test a sample bead.

Metallic Beads

GLEAMING METALLIC BEADS make wonderful accents for garments and jewelry. I have included four methods for applying metallic finishes. Read through the instructions before purchasing materials.

You can oxidize your metallic-leafed beads, as described on pages 68–69. Don't spray your beads with acrylic sealant if you plan to oxidize them.

You Will Need

For all methods:

- ♦ Rubber bands or tape
- ♦ Wide-mouth container
- ♦ Wooden beads (any size)
- ♦ Wooden skewers

Making Beads

1. Prepare wooden skewers with rubber bands or tape as described on page 15.

2. Place a wooden bead on a skewer. To apply a metallic finish, choose one of the methods on the following pages.

Composition Metal Leaf

In addition to the supplies listed on page 63, you will need:

Step 1

♦ Acrylic spray sealant

♦ Composition metal leaf (See "Resources" on page 76. Composition metal leaf is available in books of 25 sheets. Colors include gold, variegated red or green with gold, aluminum, and copper.)

♦ Small paintbrush

♦ Soft cloth or a soft bristle brush

♦ White glue, gel medium, or spray adhesive

Step 2

1. Using a small paintbrush, apply a thin layer of white glue or gel medium to the bead, or lightly spray the bead with a spray adhesive. If you are using white glue or a liquid adhesive, allow the adhesive to "set," or dry slightly, before you attempt to apply the leafing. The adhesive should feel tacky to the touch.

2. Tear off a small piece of metal leaf (enough to cover about ⅓ of the bead). Carefully press it against the adhesive-coated bead. As you apply metal leaf, blow gently on the bead. This will help remove excess leafing.

3. Using a soft cloth or bristle brush, gently pat the metal leaf in place.

Step 3

4. Repeat steps 2–3 until the bead is completely covered with leafing. If necessary, use the paintbrush to add a little more adhesive. If you are using a spray adhesive, don't try to respray the bead. Instead, spray a bit of glue on some scrap paper and use a toothpick or cotton swab to put it on the bead. Respraying makes a sticky mess!

5. Stand the skewer upright in a wide-mouth container, allow the adhesive to dry for 1 hour, then spray the bead with an acrylic sealant. The sealant keeps the metal leaf from tarnishing.

Liquid Metal Leaf

In addition to the supplies listed on page 63, you will need:

* Acrylic spray sealant
* Liquid metal leaf (gold, silver, or copper)
* Small paintbrush

1. Using a small paintbrush, paint the bead with the liquid metal leaf.

2. Stand the skewer upright in a wide-mouth container, and allow the liquid metal leaf to dry, then spray with an acrylic sealant.

Metallic Spray Paint

In addition to the supplies listed on page 63, you will need:

* Acrylic spray sealant
* Metallic spray paints
* Shoe box

Most metallic craft paints have a plastic base and only look as though they have real metal in them. If you want to oxidize your beads, use an enamel or oil-based paint, or a paint specified as *liquid gold leaf.* Acrylic- or plastic-based paints will not oxidize.

1. Apply metallic spray paint following the instructions on page 22. Remember to turn the skewer as you spray, and avoid using too much paint.

2. After the paint sets, lay the skewer across an open box until the paint is completely dry, then spray with an acrylic sealant if you don't want the bead to oxidize.

Metallic Wax

In addition to the supplies listed on page 63, you will need:

* Metallic wax (Rub and Buff, AMACO Decorator's Gilt, or Treasure Gold)
* Soft cloth
* Cotton swab

1. Using your fingers or a cotton swab, rub metallic wax on the bead.

2. Allow the wax to dry, then use a soft cloth to buff the surface.

Sheet-Metal Beads

COPPER, BRASS, AND aluminum come in thin sheets called "tooling metal or foil." This sheet metal is an ideal beadmaking material, because it's so easy to manipulate. You may also want to try copper screening.

You Will Need

- Emery paper
- Lightweight sheet metal (look for brass, copper, or aluminum tooling metal—#24 and #30 work well)
- Old scissors or metal snips
- Wooden skewers

Making Beads

1. Using old scissors or metal snips, cut a rectangle from the sheet metal. A 1" x 3" rectangle is a good size to begin with.

    If desired, smooth the sheet metal edges with emery paper. You can also cut a shape larger than your desired finished size, then fold each side in ⅛" to ¼". This makes softer, cleaner edges—a big advantage if you want to use the bead on clothing.

2. Roll a rectangle around a wooden skewer as shown. This is a lot like rolling paper beads! Don't roll the bead too tight, or it will be hard to pull it off of the skewer.

3. Slide your bead off of the skewer.

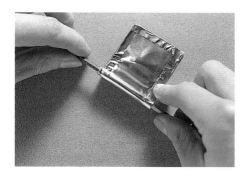

Step 1
Step 2

EXPERIMENTING

♦ Experiment with shapes other than rectangles. Try rolling triangles from the longest side up to the point.

♦ Cut a large square of sheet metal, then fold in the sides to make them smooth. Fold the metal in half several times, as if you were folding a towel. This creates a small bundle. Make the bundles any shape and size you want. Experiment with flat cut pieces to find what you like best.

♦ Enhance your beads by wrapping wire around them. Cut a long piece of wire, then wrap it around your bead or tie a bundle as though you were tying ribbon on a gift. Twist the wire on itself to secure.

Add a few beads before you twist off, just for the fun of it. Be careful to snip the wires close to the bead so they don't catch on clothing. Use tweezers to bend the ends in.

♦ Use a thin nail to punch holes in the edges of the sheet metal before rolling it. String beads on wire, then loop the wire between the holes. When you roll up the bead, it will have a frilly edge.

♦ Make buttons. Clean the metal surface of a bead with a bit of rubbing alcohol, then use E6000 adhesive to glue a small button shank to it.

Oxidized Beads

OXIDATION OCCURS WHEN a chemical interacts with oxygen to turn metal a pleasing green or blue, like the lovely coppery-green roofs we admire on old buildings. I've included two oxidation processes. The commercial version is easy and works quickly. The homemade version produces neat, unexpected colors. Read through the instructions before purchasing materials.

PATINA GREEN OR BLUE METHOD

You Will Need

- Acrylic spray sealant
- Metallic beads or found objects
- Paper towels
- Patina Green or Blue (a commercial oxidizing formula available at craft and hardware stores)
- Shallow dish
- Tongs (optional)

Making Beads

1. Place your beads in a shallow dish, then add just enough Patina solution to cover the beads. Wait 1 minute.

2. Remove the beads from the solution and place them on a folded paper towel. (You can use your fingers or tongs.) As the beads dry, the metal will begin to oxidize and turn green or blue.

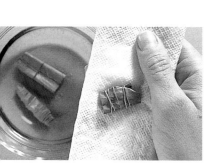

Step 1

Step 2

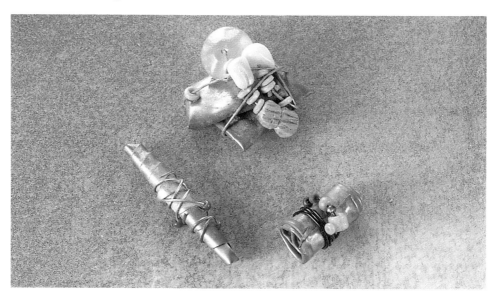

If the beads don't oxidize enough to suit you, return them to the solution for another minute, then let them dry again. Beads often oxidize more on the second or third try.

3. To stop the oxidation process, spray the dry beads with an acrylic sealant.

SALT AND VINEGAR METHOD

You Will Need

- ½ to ¾ cup vinegar
- 1 cup salt (iodized or noniodized)
- ½ cup ammonia
- Acrylic spray sealant
- Cotton swab or plastic knife
- Measuring cup and spoons
- Metallic beads or found objects
- Mixing spoon
- Shallow containers (2-cup capacity or larger) to hold solutions
- Shoe box or other container with a tight-fitting lid

Making Beads

1. Pour the salt into a small container, then slowly add the vinegar, stirring to make a paste. The paste should be thin enough to spread, but thick enough to stick to the bead surface without running. You may not need all of the vinegar.

Step 1

2. Rub the vinegar-salt paste onto the bead with a cotton swab or plastic knife. The piece does not need to be heavily coated. If it is too heavily coated, the salt will oxidize rather than the metal and the oxidation will disappear when you rinse off the salt.

4. Pour the ammonia into a shallow container. Place the container inside the shoe box, along with the beads you have coated with salt and vinegar. *Do not place the beads in the ammonia.* The ammonia does not touch the beads at any time. The fumes do the work. Cover the box with a lid.

Step 4

5. The beads begin to oxidize in 1 to 24 hours, and will continue oxidizing. Check after 6 hours. The beads will gradually turn blue or green, depending on the type of metal. When the beads are a color you like, remove them from the shoe box and gently rinse off the vinegar-salt paste with water.

6. Allow the beads to air dry. They will continue to oxidize as they dry.

7. To stop the oxidation process, spray the dry beads with an acrylic sealant.

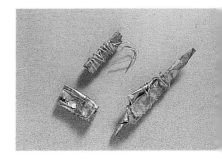
Step 5

Wire-Wrapped Beads

THERE ARE MANY kinds of wire. Look for brass, copper, cloth-covered, and plastic-coated wire. See "Resources" on page 76 for mail-order suppliers. Dick Blick sells a bag of plastic-coated wire in different colors, which is great for kids. Beware of the anodized wire sometimes sold in jewelers' supply stores. It breaks easily.

You Will Need

- Old scissors or metal snips
- Tweezers
- Wooden skewers
- Wire (24 or 30 gauge)

EXPERIMENTING

- Add beads to the wire as you wrap. Folding in the end of the wire by 1" will keep the beads from slipping off.

- Oxidize metal beads as described on pages 68–69. The oxidizing solution may alter the color of seed beads.

- Use more than one color of wire for wrapping, or braid different colors of thin wire before wrapping.

Making Beads

1. Using old scissors or metal snips, cut a 10" length of wire. Bend 1" of the wire perpendicular, so that it makes an L at one end.

2. Lay the 1" end of the wire against a wooden skewer.

3. Wrap the remaining wire around the skewer, over the tail of wire against the skewer. Don't wrap too tightly! If you do, you'll never get the bead off of the skewer.

4. Keep wrapping the wire down the skewer until you have covered the 1" section. Keep wrapping, overlapping the wire until all of it is wound around the skewer. Leave a ½" tail.

5. Pull the wire bead off the skewer. Using tweezers, tuck the tail inside the bead so that it won't catch on clothing.

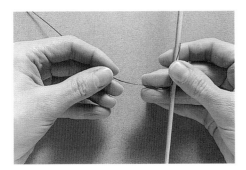

Step 2

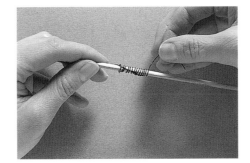

Step 4

Design Ideas

DESIGN IDEAS AND inspirations are all around us. Walk through your neighborhood and think about what you see. How do the tree branches drape? What do the stones on the street really look like? What is happening in the gardens you pass? No matter what time of year it is, you can learn something about color and shape by truly looking at things around you.

We're surrounded by commercial and graphic art. Check out colors in the stores. Look at the displays during a holiday season. Take home your visual experiences and sift through them, separating the kernels of ideas from the chaff of trivial reality!

Lastly, look at books. Not just bead books, but books on everything—artists, nature, design, ceramics. Let visual inspiration flow through you, and eventually it will settle into you and inspire you in its own unique—your own unique—way. This is the path to an enlightened, creative life, a life overflowing with abundance even when things could be going better. Seek it and you will be rewarded. Sounds like a lot to ask from a few simple beads, but it works.

Using Your Beads

YOU CAN USE your beads in all kinds of ways. Add them to clothing. (Do think through how you will attach the beads and clean the garments.) Use them to embellish fiber art. Make earrings, bracelets, necklaces, and pins. You may want to find a basic jewelry book or class for help with pin backs and earring posts and with stringing. Make tassels with beads, and use them to embellish your home furnishings. Use your beads to embellish your surroundings. When you do, you also enhance your life. Enjoy!

Resources

YOU'LL BE ABLE to find many supplies in craft and hardware stores in your area. Consider these sources for specialty items.

Clotilde, Inc.
Highway 54 West
Louisiana, MO 63353
(800) 772-2891
Sewing supplies and fabric glues

Dharma Trading Co.
PO Box 150916
San Rafael, CA 94915
(800) 542-5227
Great paints, dyes, and related products

Dick Blick
PO Box 1267
Galesburg, IL 61402-1267
(800) 828-4548
Friendly Plastic, sheet metal, wire, composition metal leaf

Edgemont Yarn Service
(606) 759-7614
Wool roving for felted beads

Nan C. Meinhardt
(847) 433-1510
Gorgeous seed and bugle beads from a talented and wonderful bead artist. Call for information.

Ornamental Resources, Inc.
Box 3010
1427 Miner Street
Idaho Springs, CO 80452
Huge selection of beads and findings

Pottery Barn
Call for catalog: (800) 922-5507
Patina solutions

Rio Grande Weavers Supply
216B Pueblo Norte
Taos, NM 87571
(800) 765-1272
Wool roving for felted beads

Universal Synergetics
16510 SW Edminston Road
 Wilsonville, OR 97070
(503) 625-2323
Great seed and bugle beads and supplies

Recommended Reading

Coles, Janet and Robert Budwig. *The Books of Beads: A Practical and Inspirational Guide to Beads and Jewelry Making.* New York: Simon and Schuster, 1990.

Dunnewold, Jane. *Complex Cloth: A Comprehensive Guide to Surface Design.* Bothell, Wash.: That Patchwork Place, 1996.

Enthoven, Jacqueline. *The Stitches of Creative Embroidery.* Rev ed. New York: Schiffer Publishing, Ltd., 1987.

Kato, Donna. *The Art of Polymer Clay: Designs and Techniques for Making Jewelry, Pottery, and Decorative Artwork.* New York: Watson-Guptill Publications, 1997.

Moss, Kathlyn and Alice Scherer. *The New Beadwork.* New York: Harry N. Abrams, Inc., 1992.

Ornament Magazine, Box 2349, San Marcos, CA 92079.

Roche, Nan. *The New Clay: Techniques and Approaches to Jewelry Making.* Rockville, Md.: Flower Valley Press, 1991.

Smith, Barbara Lee. *Celebrating the Stitch: Contemporary Embroidery of North America.* Taunton Press, 1991.

Wilson, Erica. *Erica Wilson's Embroidery Book.* New York: Charles Scribner Sons, 1973.

Index

Meet the Artist

JANE DUNNEWOLD lives in San Antonio, Texas, where she chairs the design department at the Southwest School of Art and Craft. Jane has worked as an artist with a specific interest in textiles since 1980. She shares her home with trumpet player John Carroll and daughter Zenna.

Selected Titles from Fiber Studio Press and That Patchwork Place

FIBER STUDIO PRESS

Complex Cloth: A Comprehensive Guide to Surface Design · Jane Dunnewold
Erika Carter: Personal Imagery in Art Quilts · Erika Carter
Inspiration Odyssey: A Journey of Self-Expression in Quilts · Diana Swim Wessel
The Nature of Design · Joan Colvin
Thread Magic: The Enchanted World of Ellen Anne Eddy · Ellen Anne Eddy
Velda Newman: A Painter's Approach to Quilt Design · Velda Newman with Christine Barnes

Appliqué in Bloom · Gabrielle Swain
Bargello Quilts · Marge Edie
Blockbender Quilts · Margaret J. Miller
Color: The Quilter's Guide · Christine Barnes
Colourwash Quilts · Deirdre Amsden
Freedom in Design · Mia Rozmyn
Hand-Dyed Fabric Made Easy · Adriene Buffington
Machine Needlelace and Other Embellishment Techniques · Judy Simmons
Quilted Sea Tapestries · Ginny Eckley
Watercolor Impressions · Pat Magaret & Donna Slusser
Watercolor Quilts · Pat Magaret & Donna Slusser

Many titles are available at your local quilt shop or where fine books are sold. For more information, write for a free color catalog to That Patchwork Place, Inc., PO Box 1930, Woodinville, Washington 98072-1930 USA.

U.S. and Canada, call 1-800-426-3126 for the name and location of the quilt shop nearest you.
Int'l: 1-425-483-3313 Fax: 1-425-486-7596
E-mail: info@patchwork.com
Web: www.patchwork.com